LEONARD J. ARRINGTON
MORMON HISTORY LECTURE SERIES
No. 13

WHAT'S TRUE IN MORMON HISTORY? The Contribution of Folklore to Mormon Studies

by

William A. Wilson

September 27, 2007

Sponsored by

Special Collections & Archives
Merrill Library
Utah State University
Logan, Utah

ISBN 978-0-87421-717-9
Distributed by
Utah State University Press
Logan, Utah 84322-7800

Introduction

F. Ross Peterson

The establishment of a lecture series honoring a library's special collections and a donor to that collection is unique. Utah State University's Merrill-Cazier Library houses the personal and historical collection of Leonard J. Arrington, a renowned scholar of the American West. As part of Arrington's gift to the university, he requested that the university's historical collection become the focus for an annual lecture on an aspect of Mormon history. Utah State agreed to the request and in 1995 inaugurated the annual Leonard J. Arrington Mormon History Lecture.

Utah State University's Special Collections and Archives is ideally suited as the host for the lecture series. The state's land grant university began collecting records very early, and in the 1960s became a major depository for Utah and Mormon records. Leonard and his wife Grace joined the USU faculty and family in 1946, and the Arringtons and their colleagues worked to collect original diaries, journals, letters, and photographs.

Although trained as an economist at the University of North Carolina, Arrington became a Mormon historian of international repute. Working with numerous colleagues, the Twin Falls, Idaho, native produced the classic *Great Basin Kingdom: An Economic History of the Latter-day Saints* in 1958. Utilizing available collections at USU, Arrington embarked on a prolific publishing and editing career. He and his close ally, Dr. S. George Ellsworth, helped organize the Western History Association, and they created the *Western Historical Quarterly* as the scholarly voice of the WHA. While serving with Ellsworth as editor of the new journal, Arrington also helped both the Mormon History Association and the independent journal *Dialogue* get established.

One of Arrington's great talents was to encourage and inspire other scholars or writers. While he worked on biographies or institutional histories, he employed many young scholars as researchers. He fostered many careers as well as arranged for the publication of numerous books and articles.

In 1973, Arrington accepted appointments as the official historian of the Church of Jesus Christ of Latter-day Saints and the Lemuel Redd Chair of Western History at Brigham Young University. More and more Arrington focused on Mormon, rather than economic, historical topics. His own career flourished with the publication of *The Mormon Experience*, co-authored with Davis Bitton, and *American Moses: A Biography of Brigham Young*. He and his staff produced many research papers and position papers for the LDS Church as well. Nevertheless, tension developed over the historical process, and Arrington chose to move full time to BYU with his entire staff. The Joseph Fielding Smith Institute of History was established, and Leonard continued to mentor new scholars as well as publish biographies. He also produced a very significant two-volume study, *The History of Idaho*.

After Grace Arrington passed away, Leonard married Harriet Horne of Salt Lake City. They made the decision to deposit the vast Arrington collection of research documents, letters, files, books, and journals at Utah State University. The Leonard J. Arrington Historical Archives is part of the university's Special Collections. The Arrington Lecture Committee works with Special Collections to sponsor the annual lecture.

William A. (Bert) Wilson holds a Ph.D. in folklore from Indiana University. He has taught at Indiana University, UCLA, Utah State University, the University of Oregon, and Brigham Young University, where he is currently Humanities Professor Emeritus of Folklore and Literature. At USU he served as the Director of the Folklore Program and developed the annual Fife Folklore Conference. He also helped develop the Fife Folklore Archive and was instrumental in incorporating that archive into the Merrill Library's holdings. At BYU he served as chair of the English Department, as director of the Charles Redd Center for Western Studies, and as director of the BYU Folklore Archives. He has served as editor of *Western Folklore*, as president of the Utah Folklore Society, as president of the Association for Mormon Letters, as a member of the executive board of the American Folklore Society, as a member of the board of directors of the Utah Arts Council, as chair of the Utah Folk Arts Panel, as chair of the board of trustees of the Western Folklife Center, and as chair of the Folk Arts Panel of the National Endowment for the Arts.

His research interests have taken him to Finland, to the American West, and to his own Mormon culture. He has done fieldwork for the American Folklife Center of the Library of Congress, documenting contemporary folklore and ranching customs in Paradise Valley, Nevada, and has consulted regularly on public folklore programs. He is the author of *Folklore and Nationalism in Modern Finland (Kalevala ja kansallisuusaate)*, which won two national awards, the Gustave O. Arlt Award in the Humanities from the Council of Graduate Schools in the United States and the second place award in the University of Chicago Folklore Prize Competition. He has published over eighty articles on religious folklore, on folk narrative, on Finnish folklore, and on the history of folklore study. He has twice received the Morris S. Rosenblatt Award for the best general interest article published in the *Utah Historical Quarterly*. He is the 1997 recipient of the Grace Arrington Award for Historical Excellence, the 1998 recipient of Utah's Governor's Award in the Arts, the 2002 recipient of the American Folklore Society's Americo Paredes Prize for "outstanding community engagement," and the 2002 recipient of the Mormon History Association's Leonard J. Arrington Award for "a distinctive contribution to the cause of Mormon history." In 2003 the Brigham Young Folklore Archives were renamed the William A. Wilson Folklore Archives. A collection of his essays, *The Marrow of Human Experience*, was recently published by Utah State University Press.

What's True in Mormon History?

The Contribution of Folklore to Mormon Studies

It's an honor to deliver the annual Leonard J. Arrington address. In 1985, I published a fairly nondescript little article entitled "'We Did Everything Together': Farming Customs of the Mountainwest" in *Northwest Folklore*, a journal with a very limited subscription list.[1] None of my folklore colleagues ever commented on the piece, probably because few of them had ever seen it. But, to my great surprise, shortly after the article had appeared in print, I received a friendly note from Leonard Arrington praising the article and recounting how my experiences growing up in Idaho farm country paralleled his own. And it was ever thus. Until the day he died Leonard continued to encourage me along the way.

In spite of my positive experiences with Leonard, the task that lies before me this evening is a daunting one. All twelve lecturers who have occupied this podium before me have been historians. I am a folklorist. I have always believed that folklorists and historians, as well as scholars from other disciplines, ought to cooperate more often than they usually do. This evening I'll attempt to correct here two misconceptions about folklore that sometimes make this cooperation more difficult than it needs to be. In doing so I'll try to explain why those of us who take the subject seriously believe that folklore research should play an important part of any program devoted to the study of Mormon culture.

But first, to make sure we are all on the same page, I had better begin with a definition of the materials folklorists work with. We consider folklore to be that part of our culture that we transmit through time (from age to age) and through space (from place to place), not by formal instruction or the written word, but in face-to-face encounters with other people through the processes of oral transmission or customary example. That is, a father or mother will tell a child a story of hardships encountered by pioneer ancestors as they crossed the plains; the child will, in turn, one day tell the same story to his or her own children. Or a young girl may help her mother stitch a pedigree chart onto a genealogy quilt and then will one day make her own quilts with her own daughter at her elbow. Or a group of older scouts on a campout will send tenderfoots in the group on a snipe hunt. The next year these young men, now experienced scouters, will initiate the next crop of tenderfoots with another snipe hunt, and all will be drawn more tightly into a cohesive unit.

As these examples suggest, the materials we collect and study include things we make with words (verbal lore), things we make with our hands (material lore), and things we make with our actions (customary lore). Because I come from a background in literature, I have been most interested in things we make with words and they will be my primary focus this evening. Further, from the broad field of verbal lore I will speak mostly about legends, stories the narrators generally believe to be true. You should remember, however, that one must study all forms of Mormon folklore to achieve a comprehensive view of Mormon life.

Because these cultural artifacts we call folklore depend, for their survival and dissemination, on the spoken word or on observation and imitation, they will often migrate well beyond their places of origin and will in the process spin off numerous variant forms. Nonetheless, different versions of a single form will be identifiable as related to each other by their internal structure. For example, stories of the Three Nephites, those ancient American disciples of Christ believed by Mormons to still be walking the earth, will, no matter what the details of individual stories, almost always have the same narrative structure: someone has a spiritual or physical problem, a stranger appears from nowhere, the stranger solves the problem, the stranger disappears, usually miraculously. Similarly, no matter what the overall patterns of several log cabin quilts, they can be identified as the same type because of the structural design of their individual blocks.

The trouble with this definition, so far, is that it focuses on "things" and leaves out "people"—the folk. People are always more important than things. Our goal in folklore research is, or should be, to understand the people who make the things: the singer of songs, the teller of stories; the creator of quilts, the preparer of ethnic foods; the practitioners of wedding celebrations, the players of pranks. The first misconception many people have about folklore, then, is a misunderstanding about who these people, the folk, actually are.

Serious folklore study began in Europe in the nineteenth century—on the continent under the inspiration of romantic nationalism and in England under the impulse of the idea of progress and of evolutionary anthropology. The romantic nationalists considered the folklore, which eager collectors were bringing to public attention, to be relics, or survivals, from an earlier Golden Age; the evolutionists, on the other hand, considered this same lore to be survivals not from a glorious past but from a savage age of cultural development. Though divided on questions of folklore's ultimate origins, advocates of both these schools shared a number of views. Both believed that folklore had survived in and could be found only among the rural peasant classes who had remained relatively untouched by education and by the more sophisticated and cosmopolitan life in the cities. Both saw folklore as a tool for reconstructing the past—for the romantic nationalists a glorious past that they hoped to revive and for the evolutionists a savage and barbaric past that they believed most of the race had happily, and forever, left behind. Neither school would have given any credence to the notion that folklore might help us understand the dynamics of the present or of the recent past, and both schools, therefore, would have found quite ridiculous any attempt to use folklore to better understand contemporary individuals or social communities.

Almost all serious folklorists have long ago abandoned these nineteenth century concepts. But on occasion one still finds them at play in the work of some, but certainly not all, historians These historians still consider the people who keep folklore alive to be simple, unlettered country folk; and they view this lore as quaint customs and usages, survivals from an earlier way of thinking in the evolution of culture. Operating from these outmoded concepts, these scholars neglect, or do not see, the folklore that is all around them and thus deny themselves opportunity to enhance their understanding of the materials and especially the people they study.

For example, Jon Butler, the prominent author of *Awash in a Sea of Faith: Christianizing the American People*, published in 1990 by Harvard University Press, writes:

Significant evidence suggests that the folklorization of magic occurred as much in America as in England. As in England, colonial magic and occultism did not so much disappear everywhere as they disappeared amòng certain social classes and became confined to poorer, more marginal segments of early American Society.[2]

No nineteenth-century English evolutionary anthropologist could have said it better. According to this point of view, as the majority of the population evolved, or progressed, out of the darkness of the past, elements of an earlier folk mentality supposedly persisted among uneducated, marginal, and lower class individuals. These same ideas can be found in the writings of some Mormon historians who study the treasure-seeking practices of Joseph Smith.[3]

Closely akin to this evolutionary view, but not necessarily tied to it, is the notion that folklore consists primarily of old things born in earlier times: old stories, old recipes, old games. Consider the following story:

> I am going to tell about an experience that my grandmother had and told my dad. It happened when she was crossing the plains, after coming from England. I believe she was a widow and she had a lot of children. She was crossing the plains in a covered wagon. She was alone at this time with her family—a wheel broke and caused a delay in their progress. It looked for awhile as though there was no way to mend the broken wheel. Then all of a sudden, out of nowhere, came a man. He offered great assistance and finally, through his help, the wheel was fixed. When she turned around to thank this man, he had disappeared—to where, she didn't know. For the land was very flat and there was no place he could have gone without her seeing him for quite some time. So she has told my dad, her son, that she thought that this was one of the Three Nephites that came to help her during her trouble on the plains moving west.[4]

Clearly, this is an older story, a story about the pioneer era that many church members believe to be the seat of most Mormon folklore. But now consider this story:

> Some good friends of mine were going from Southern Utah to the Salt Lake Temple. As they were traveling they had a blowout and were forced to stop and repair it. They were driving behind schedule and were in somewhat of a hurry. They had just begun to repair the tire when a peculiar looking old, white-haired gentleman walked up to them. He said very little but began helping them. Upon completion of the job, my friend turned to put his tools away. After doing so he turned to thank the fellow. He was gone. The road was straight and level for several miles; the

surrounding fields were flat and barren. No cars had passed since they had been stopped. He had apparently disappeared.[5]

In the second of these stories, the broken wagon wheel becomes a blown-out tire. Otherwise, there is little difference between them. In both a mysterious stranger, thought to be one of the Three Nephites, assists a family whose vehicle has failed them.

The settings and modes of transportation in stories like these may change as we move from the pioneer past to the present, but what remains the same is the comforting possibility that divine help is available to those who need it. And it is that comforting possibility of divine help, in both the past and the present, that was and still is the generating force behind the stories. I am often asked to speak to small groups about Mormon folklore, the expectation being that I will talk about pioneers. This is so because those making the requests fail to recognize that the stories they tell about their own lives may also be folklore. As Sterling McMurrin has noted, our own activities can become "so commonplace and habitual" that we forget to pay them proper heed when we compare them to practices in the past.[6]

At one time the principal investigator of the Nephite legend, Hector Lee, argued that as the harshness of pioneer life lessened and as church members increased in sophistication, the Nephite stories would gradually disappear. The facts, I believe, are otherwise. Lee based his 1949 study, *The Three Nephites: The Substance and Significance of the Legend in Folklore,* on 150 narratives.[7] In recent years, my students and I have collected 1,500 Nephite stories—some of them from the pioneer past but many growing out of challenges church members face in the modern world. It is possible, of course, that the Nephite stories may one day disappear, but if they do, they will be replaced by others just as remarkable and just as faith promoting as the Nephite stories. So long as church members continue to believe in that "comforting possibility" of divine protection, new stories, no matter what their form, will emerge.

Who are the folk, then? We are—all of us in this room. In the social groups to which we belong—religious, immigrant, ethnic, occupational, age, family—we generate and transmit folklore about our lives because that is the way we have, as human beings, to deal with recurring human problems in traditional human ways.

The second misconception the general public has about folklore is that it is untrue. We have all heard the dismissive statement, "Oh, that story is just folklore," meaning that it's not true and that we can dismiss it, therefore, as of no consequence. This misconception is partly the fault of some of my fellow folklorists, whose principal joy in life seems to lie in debunking other people's stories without ever contemplating why these people relate their stories and what we might learn about them and their social groups by paying heed not just to *what* they say, but to *why* they say it. Leonard Arrington noted once that whether an account "is literally true or not, it is still true"—or to paraphrase, "Just because something didn't happen doesn't mean it's not true."[8] For me, the issue is not really what is true in Mormon folklore but rather the variety of ways in which that lore can be true. In what follows, I will discuss some of these ways and comment on what these truths can contribute to our study of Mormon culture, especially the culture of lay members in the routines of everyday life. It is this emphasis on the common people that puts Mormon folklore research in harmony with the new social history, which as the past president of the American Historical Association, Eric Foner, has noted, has "focused historians' attention on the experiences of ordinary men and women" rather than on society's movers and shakers.[9]

One of the ways folklore can be true is that it gives an accurate picture of what the people believe to be true. This is not to say that what they believe cannot at times square with actual historical reality—what really happened in the past. For example, Norwegian folklorist Brynjulf Alver demonstrated that a local Norwegian legend "had preserved precise information about an event that occurred a thousand years ago—the death of a knight who "had been crushed by an avalanche as he went riding by."[10] Two American archaeologists, David M. Pendergast and Clement W. Meighan, collected from the Paiute Indians of southern Utah oral traditions about a Puebloid people who had once occupied the area with them and had then moved away. The stories squared with archaeological evidence from eight hundred years in the past, giving accurate accounts of economic institutions, material culture, physical stature of the people, and intertribal relations. The Indians knew more about the archaeological sites than their white neighbors, said the authors, because "it is their land, they have been here for thirty generations or more, their ancestors saw these communities when they were living villages, and the old people talked about it to their young."[11] And the Scottish folklorist, David D. Buchan has shown that the ballad, "The Battle of Harlaw," which recounts the battle in 1411 between the highland and lowland Scots, has preserved the details of that battle more accurately than have the sober histories."[12]

I could add further examples of folklore squaring with historical reality. More often than not, however, there will be a disconnect between what the people believe happened and what really took place. This being the case, one might ask, why should we spend any time studying something that is not demonstrably true? Speaking to this issue, our Norwegian folklorist, Alver, writes:

> The "truth" of legends . . . is not identical with the "truth" of legal documents and history books, and official documents themselves are not necessarily "objective" reports. In many instances we should consider them the representation of one view of an event. Legend tradition constitutes another view. . . . Legends reveal the reactions and reflections of the common folk, their impressions, experiences, and their explanation and evaluation of events that are important to them.[13]

Why is it important to know the common people's views of events? Because people are motivated and moved to action not by what really happened but by what they believe happened. If they believe the stories, whether true or false, the beliefs will produce social consequences in their lives, and it is these consequences that are our concerns. Some of you will remember events that took place in Utah during late 1969 and early 1970, during the months preceding the April General Conference of the LDS Church. At that time, African Americans had not yet been granted priesthood privileges and the church had come under sharp attack for its racial policies. At the same time, apocryphal prophecies about racial wars and bloodshed to precede the last days spread widely through the area. As a result, many Mormons became convinced that Black-White conflict was imminent and would reach its peak during the April conference. Stories that justified this belief spread like wildfire throughout the Intermountain region. The following account is typical:

> Did you hear about the kids who were on their way to California and got jumped by some Blacks as they stopped for something to eat? I think it was in Nevada somewhere. Anyway, they were going to eat. They stopped and were jumped by some Blacks who happened to see their BYU sticker on their car. They messed up the car and drove it off the road and then beat up the guys and did who knows what to the girls.[14]

Other stories claimed that cars with Utah license plates were not safe out of state, that carloads of Blacks were on the way to Salt Lake, that the Black Panthers were sneaking into the city with guns, that all the hotels around the temple were filled with Blacks, that the Lake Shore Ward Sacrament Meeting had been interrupted by Blacks, that the SDS and the Black Panthers planned to blow up Mountain Dell Reservoir, that Black children were to sell candy bars laced with broken glass, that two bombs had been discovered on Temple Square, and that Blacks would storm Temple Square during conference.

Conference came and went—peacefully. The stories proved groundless, or at least non-verifiable. But in the days before the conference they had a powerful influence on many who believed them. Some formed neighborhood defense groups; others, one of my neighbors among them, stored guns and ammunition in preparation for the coming conflict; and some who had planned to travel from elsewhere to attend the conference remained home. And in all these instances it was not actual history, verifiable accounts of what had really happened, but *folk history*, what the people believed had happened and was happening, that governed their lives. We ignore this kind of history at our peril.

Another way in which folklore is true, as anthropologist Franz Boas taught us a century ago, is that it mirrors the culture of the people who possess it. In 1910, abandoning the evolutionary approach of the English anthropologists, Boas wrote in a study of Tsimshian Indian narratives:

> It is obvious that in the tales of a people those incidents of the everyday life that are of importance to them will appear either incidentally or as the basis of a plot. Most of the references to the mode of life of the people will be an accurate reflection of their habits. The development of the plot of the story . . . will, on the whole, exhibit clearly what is considered right and wrong.[16]

In other words, what is in the culture, will also be in the folklore. Mormons, like all people, tell stories about those things that interest them most and are most important to them. The church is awash in stories. Members talk constantly of hardships faithfully endured by pioneer ancestors, of present-day persecutions, of missions, of conversions, of God's interventions in individuals' lives, of admiration for and sometimes frustration with church authorities, of the day-to-day delights and sorrows of church membership. If we want to understand Mormon hearts and minds, if we want to know their hopes, fears, dreams, and anxieties, we must know their stories. This is so for the simple reason that folk narratives depend on the spoken word for their survival. Each individual LDS member is in some ways different from all other LDS members. We should therefore avoid characterizing anyone as a stereotypical Mormon—I have never met such a creature. Still, if a story does not appeal to a sufficient number of church members to keep it alive, if it does not somehow relate to what I have called the group's value center[17] —a consensus center of attitude and belief that ties all members of the group together—it will either be altered by the tellers, often unconsciously, to make it conform to that value center or it will disappear. Those stories that continue to be told can serve, therefore, as a barometer of the group's principal concerns at any given time. For example, though the Nephite stories in my collection tell a multitude of different tales, they have tended in recent times to cluster around three major themes: missionary work, family history research, and welfare. As many of you will know, these are the three points of emphasis of the Priesthood Correlation Program initiated in 1964. To the exhortation of church authorities have been added the witnesses of the ancient Nephite apostles, testifying to the faithful of the church's program and prompting them to obey its dictates.

Implicit in Boas's statement that folk narratives mirror what a group considers right and wrong is the notion that the lore also teaches this knowledge. In other words, it fills an instructional function. As Barre Toelken notes, "Folklore constitutes a basic and important educative and expressive setting in which individuals learn how to see, act, respond, and express themselves by the empirical observation of close human interactions and expressions in their immediate society."[18] Firemen who tell new hires stories of past fires, are not just titillating them with exciting narratives; they are teaching them what to do and what not do if they want to remain alive in future fires.[19] A senior LDS missionary who tells his greenie companion about an errant missionary who decided to test his powers by ordaining a post to the priesthood and then was zapped by a bolt of lighting, a story well known in the mission field,[20] is not just relating an intriguing story; he is instructing the greenie not to behave in a sacrilegious manner if he wants to avoid the errant missionary's fate. The important point to remember here is that folk narratives, like the following well-traveled story, both mirror the storytellers' culture and function in that culture in important ways, satisfying the tellers' own ends and meeting their own needs.

A young married couple with a four-year-old daughter had recently moved into a new home by a stream. One day they had an opportunity to attend the temple to do [vicarious] work for the dead. During the session, the mother had a terrible feeling that wouldn't go away. She decided that when the session was over she would go home. When they arrived at their home, there was a police car and an ambulance in the drive way. They jumped from their car and ran into the home to find the baby sitter very upset. She told them that the daughter had disappeared and she found her doll on the bank of the stream. The mother noticed wet footprints in the hall going up the stairs. She followed them to a bedroom closet. She opened the door and found the girl dripping wet asleep. She woke the girl up and asked her what happened. The girl said she was playing by the stream and fell in. "This nice lady in a white dress helped me and brought me upstairs. She gave me this piece of paper and told me to give it to only you, Mom." The mother looked at the paper and read the name. It was the name of the woman she just did work for at the temple that day.[21]

To believing Mormons, this story speaks many messages. It encourages them to persist in the search for their ancestral roots; it testifies to the validity of temple ordinances; it suggests that God is a caring God who will protect them in time of need; it stresses the importance of the family and strengthens family ties; and it gives them hope that these ties will continue beyond this life. The story, then, both reflects and affirms church teaching. Its messages are brought forcefully home by an artistic performance designed to move listeners to action and made all the more powerful by the narrative symmetry in which two lives are saved at the same moment—the physical life of the young girl and the eternal life of the lady in white, the mother serving as the link between the two. It is, therefore, an important artifact for anyone interested not just in the Mormon past, but also in Mormon social organization, Mormon belief, and Mormon creative expression.

The concept I mentioned above, that each group has its own value center, is crucially important in understanding the nature of the "truth" mirrored in folklore. Two stories should illustrate this point. In the first story, two missionaries serving in Canada had a frightening experience, which they interpreted as an encounter with an evil spirit. They told the story to only a few others. One of the two recorded the incident in his journal. A few years later, now a student at BYU in my folklore class, he chose as his term project to collect stories from individuals recently returned from his own mission. Much to his surprise, he collected several versions of his own story. He and his companion had done nothing wrong, but in the stories he collected they had been converted into rule-breaking missionaries. One informant stated: "I think that it was late at night and that the elders hadn't been livin' the mission rules very well and they were sort of apostate elders anyhow . . . kind of the haughty kind . . . That sort of thing never happens to ya if you're livin' your religion." In a few short years the account of this experience had been filtered through the value center of the missionary group, changing in the process into a story reflecting the belief that disobedient missionaries subject themselves to the power of Satan and becoming also a tale that encourages other missionaries not to get involved in like behavior.[22]

The second story I heard in 1982 in a talk by Leonard Arrington in which he described conditions in arid southern Utah, where the little rain that does fall often comes down in cloud bursting torrents that wash away crops and irrigation systems. To illustrate his point he told of a young lady from southern Utah who offered a public prayer for rain. She implored the Lord not to send "a slip-slashing, gulley-washing" storm but to bless them instead with "a nice, gentle, drizzle-drazzle, ground-soaking" rain.[23]

The story immediately set bells ringing in my head. In a class I was teaching, I had recently assigned my students to read Zora Neal Hurston's *Mules and Men*. From this collection of African American folklore, we had read the following story:

> Well, it come a famine and all de crops was dried up and Brother John was ast to pray He had prayed for rain last year and it had rained, so all de white folks 'sembled at they church and called on Brother John to pray again, so he got down and prayed: "Now Lord, we want some rain. Our crops is all burning up and we'd like a little rain. But I don't mean for you to come in a hell of a storm like you did last year—kicking up a racket like black folks at a barbecue. I want you to come calm and easy."[24]

About this same time I had collected some Danish dialect stories from my good friend Woodruff Thompson. A dialect story is a popular form of American folklore in which the tellers mimic the fractured English of their immigrant parents and grandparents. Having grown up among

Danish immigrants in Ephraim, Utah, Woodruff had accumulated a rich store of narratives like the following tale in which an old Dane not only prays to the Lord for rain to save the crops but bargains with him as well

> Now, Lord, we do vant you to send us rain. But ve vant it to be a yentle rain–a long, yentle rain. Ve do not vant a cloudburst dat vil bring a flood out of de canyon to put mud and boulders in our gardens and fields. And, Lord, ve do not vant a big hail storm like de vun you sent last year dat knocked all the heads off de hveat yost ven it was ripening. Ve want a nice, yentle rain. And, Lord, ve know dat if you vil tink of it, you vil see the reasonableness of vat ve ask, and how it vil be an advantage to bote us and to you. Because if we do not get the yentle rain dat vil safe de crops, neither vil you get your tithing.[25]

In this instance we are dealing not with the re-creation of an actual event to square with a group's value center, as in the evil spirit story, but with a well-traveled tale that moves from cultural group to cultural group, each time being filtered through the value centers and cultural environments of the different groups. You will remember that the supplicator in the African American version of the story was named John. In African American lore, the story is part of a large cycle of "Old Marster and John" tales[26] in which the slave John, superior in intellect and cunning, gets the better of his white masters. It is only logical that needing rain, they would turn to him for help. As the story moved into the immigrant lore of Ephraim, Utah, and was once again filtered through this group's consensus value center and cultural environment, the petitioner's language changed to Danish dialect and the LDS concept of blessings resulting from paying tithing was introduced. But the change was much more significant than that. When I told the story to my friend Darwin Hayes, who had grown up on a farm in Bear Lake country, he responded. "To us those are just stories, but back then they were the facts of life." What were those facts? That the weather often did destroy crops, that there was no welfare system in place to save a family that lost its crops, and that loss of crops could mean starvation. Pretty severe facts. How did people survive those circumstances? Partly by telling humorous stories like this one that mitigated the harshness of their lives and gave them the strength and the resiliency to get up in the morning and keep struggling ahead. To dismiss either of these narratives, as just idle tales with no historical significance would be folly. They are important cultural artifacts that reveal truths we cannot always get in other ways.

Changes in the lore also occur not just when stories move from cultural group to cultural group but as the culture changes within a group across time. From pioneer days to the present, few themes have been more popular in Mormon folklore than that of divine protection of missionaries. Such stories give courage to the missionaries and provide comfort to their families back home. The following story comes from the pioneer era, from a time when missionaries traveled without purse or script and had to take lodging wherever they could find it:

> Two missionaries found a home where the owner was willing to let them stay for the night. Some people found out, and soon a mob of angry people was at the house with pitchforks and lanterns, demanding that the missionaries come out before they burn the house. The elders came out, and ropes were put around their necks. They then were marched to a grove of trees Just as the mob was ready to pull the ropes, every single lantern went out. There was no light anywhere, no moon and no stars. Quickly the elders took off the ropes and began to run. But it was hard because of all the trees and shrubs. They fell to the ground and didn't move a muscle. The men in the mob searched all around for them, but they couldn't find them even though their feet were right by the missionaries' faces.[27]

In the following widely-known contemporary story, the scene changes from a rural to an urban setting, and the angry mob becomes a street gang who use chains and knives rather than pitchforks. The miracle of the lamps all suddenly extinguishing is replaced by a miracle even more remarkable:

> [These missionaries] were in a bad part of town. And they were in teaching a family, and when they came out there was a gang waiting to beat up these missionaries. And the missionaries got really scared and ran to the car and got in it . . . , and it wouldn't start. Meanwhile, the guys with the chains and the knives were starting to get closer and closer to the car. So they got real scared, and the one says, "Well, let's have a prayer." So they said the prayer and turned on the ignition, and sure enough, the car started up and they took off. And they got about five or ten miles away or so—anyway they decided to find out why the car wouldn't start, and they got out, and they opened the hood, and there's no battery.[28]

The missionaries in both these stories were males, elders. That's what one would expect because until recent times most missionaries were male. There were females, sister missionaries, earlier but they did not comprise a critical mass large enough to generate a body of folklore. That has all changed now. Most missionaries are still males, but large numbers of females have joined their ranks. The changes that have occurred in the divine protection narratives told by them take on a different coloring. Consider the following story:

> These two sister missionaries were out tracting one day, and they came onto this deserted house, and they didn't know this but the guy living in there had escaped from prison. He was in prison for killing women, and the women he had killed were right there in the 21–23 age group. Well, they knocked and he wasn't interested, so they went on their way. Well they saw a flyer or something that showed his picture and said that he was wanted, so they turned him in and identified him. And when he was taken into the police department they asked him why he hadn't killed those two girls that had come tracting, because they were just the age group that he was always killing. And he said there was no way that he was going to even touch those girls because they had three big guys with swords standing behind them. So he just wanted to get rid of them as quickly as possible because those big guys with swords would have killed him if he had touched the girls.[29]

The burly protectors of the sister missionaries are generally thought to be the Three Nephites, or sometimes they are simply called angels or divine personages. In some versions of the story the killer is also a rapist.

About the same time I became interested in this story a colleague from North Carolina sent me the following story submitted by one of his folklore students:

> It was told to me, a girl was coming home from the library. . . . Warren Wilson is a private school; I think it's run by Methodist or something and they have a lot of shaded little trails and stuff that are very dangerous, but the story is true because a minister . . . told it—that there was a girl walking on the path by herself coming from the library, and you know happy-go-lucky, singing and praying. There was a guy on the path who was just standing there. . . . And she was on this path and she walked past this guy. He didn't say anything to her or anything; he just left her alone, but hours later or a day later she heard of a girl who was raped and the girl gave a description of this guy and she remembered seeing this guy on the path. So she went to the police department and asked for permission to speak to the guy. . . . She asked him, "Why?" She said, "I was on this path; I was by myself; why didn't you attack me?" He said, "Because there was another person with you." She said, "No, I was by myself." He goes, "But yes, there was a person with you, a huge person." And from this story we

get that that could be her Holy Comforter that was walking with her. So, if you just wish in the name of Jesus, He will be there.[30]

Here we see further evidence that stories can not only spin off different versions within the cultural groups that tell them; they can also cross societal boundaries and be transformed to fit the cultural contours, the value centers, of different groups. I suppose one could argue that the Mormon and Methodist versions of this story are of independent origin. The Lord, after all, loves Mormon and Methodist girls equally well, but the stories are too structurally similar to make that very likely. One might argue that the same story occurring in different groups is adequate evidence that the story is not true and is therefore of little scholarly importance. But the stories have been far too popular, especially among young people of missionary age, to ignore their cultural significance. In 1994 I gave a talk at the former Ricks College. The auditorium, which seated about 900 people, had standing room only. I told this story and then asked how many had heard it. I would estimate that at least eighty percent of those present raised their hands.

The story does more than simply reflect the fact that the number of sister missionaries is increasing and that, as a result, female missionaries now take a larger part in missionary lore. They reveal a more important truth. To understand this truth we must step outside the texts. Of the thirty-seven versions of the story I have studied closely the earliest was collected in 1985, and in none of the accounts was the action described thought to have occurred before 1980, a fact reflecting the recent origin of the story. Twenty-four of the stories were collected from women, suggesting that this is a story especially meaningful to them. Sister missionaries know that because they cannot hold the priesthood held by the male elders and because they have not been encouraged to serve missions as strongly as have the elders, they will sometimes be scorned and held in less regard as missionaries. When elders do tell this story, they again stress the possibility of divine protection in the face of danger. Sisters stress the same possibility, but some of them also see in the story a validation of their roles as missionaries. One of them said, "Since it specifically concerned sisters, [it] helped calm some of my fears. The fact that the story was about sisters instead of elders showed me that the Lord was just as concerned about the few as the many."[31] Another said that the mission president's wife had told her the story to remind her "that God protects sisters, as well as the elders."[32] If sisters and elders were held in equal regard by all, such a reminder would, of course, not be necessary.

The stories emerging here are typical of narratives emerging across the full spectrum of missionary life. As changes in the missionary system continue to occur, influencing gender roles and sometimes inspiring gender conflicts, missionary lore will remain a sensitive indicator of missionary attitudes and beliefs, helping us take the pulse of missionary life. Similarly, as changes occur in the larger church, the full range of Mormon folklore accumulating in folklore archives will help us keep our fingers on the pulse of Mormon life.

In the years following Franz Boas's declaration that folklore could serve as a mirror for a people's culture, a number of his students followed the course charted by their teacher in their own work. For example, in her 1935 publication, *Zuni Mythology*, Boas's former student Ruth Benedict, sounding very much like Boas himself, wrote: "The agreement between the conduct of contemporary life and the picture of life in the folktales is very close. The roles of men and women in Zuni life, the role of the priesthoods, the conduct of sex life, the concern with witchcraft, are all faithfully indicated." And she argued that through the processes of adoption and cultural adaptation I have described above European tales borrowed by the Zuni "that are popular or have been told for some time or are retold by a good narrator often mirror the details of Zuni life to the last degree."[33] But as Benedict collected and studied Zuni narratives, she observed also that not all of them fit the Boasian model. "It has always been obvious to students of every theoretical persuasion, she said, that folklore tallied with culture and yet did not tally with it."[34] She gave as a striking example the fact that while Zuni culture is "thoroughly monogamous," the characters in Zuni narratives constantly practiced polygamy.[35] In other words, in this instance what was in the culture was not in the folklore, a seeming contradiction of Boas's mirror of culture concept.

This same contradiction occurs in a good bit of Mormon folklore. Consider the following narrative, from the days when individual congregations had to raise money to pay for the construction of their buildings:

> A bishop who was conducting a church building fund in his ward preached a sermon from the pulpit one time about being blessed for contributing to the building fund. After his sermon, a member came up to him and said, "Bishop, that was a damned fine sermon." The bishop replied, "Brother, you had better watch the swearing." The member

continued, "Yes, sir, Bishop, that was such a damned fine sermon that I gave an extra $650 for the building fund." The bishop then said, "Yes brother, it takes a hell of a lot of money to build a church."[36] Now bishops are not, for expedient reasons, supposed to sacrifice the principles it is their duty to inculcate in their ward members, but this one does. Similarly, in the spate of stories church members tell about J. Golden Kimball, this crusty old church leader not only sprinkles his speech full of hells and damns; he irrelevantly knocks the props out from under higher, more sour and dour authorities church members are expected to honor. For instance, a senior church authority once self-righteously scolded Kimball for swearing, saying, "Why I'd rather commit adultery than swear!" Kimball responded, in his high-pitched voice, "Wouldn't we all, brother, wouldn't we all?"[37] Clearly the actions in the J. Golden Kimball stories do not mirror the behaviors of committed church members.

One of the best examples of characters in Mormon narratives acting contrary to accepted behavioral norms comes from the mission fields. One of the most popular missionary stories (known in virtually every mission field) is one my friend John Harris and I collected in the late 60's as we began gathering the folklore of Mormon missionaries, an endeavor that has lasted until the present. The first night we began collecting we were told a story we have heard many times since then—we have over one hundred versions of the story and could have collected many more. The following are two typical examples:

> [Two missionaries] had been working out on these tiny Islands in Denmark far away from the Mission Home. One of these elders was rich. The World Series was playing in the states and they really wanted to see it. So they decided they would take two weeks off and fly there. They set it up with their landlady that she would mail in their reports that they made up in advance. But she got mixed up and mailed the second one in first and the first one in second. And the Mission President found out and he met them at the airport and sent them home.[38]

> Two missionaries were stationed in Zambia and were doing their normal missionary work. After a while they decided to split and take off into the Congo. Their chapel was only forty miles from the Congo, and Leopoldville, where all the revolutionary excitement was going on, was not too much further away. So they devised a plan–to make out their reports to mission headquarters two weeks in advance and give them to their landlady, who in turn would send one in each week at an appointed

time. By this the missionaries would have two free weeks to venture into the wilds of the Congo. All this would have gone well, except the stupid landlady sent the report for the second week in first and the report for the first week second. That spilled the tomatoes, and the mission president caught them.[39]

Lest anyone be overly concerned that Mormon missionaries around the globe are taking unauthorized vacations when they should be diligently engaged in proselytizing, I should point out that this story, like the story of the sister missionaries and the rapist and many other supposedly "Mormon" stories, has had elsewhere its origin. In his history of Harvard, published in 1937, historian Samuel Eliot Morison tells that in 1886 the university adopted a policy of "discretionary supervision" to monitor student attendance. Says Morison:

> "Discretionary supervision" meant in practice that upperclassmen could cut classes at will; and term-time trips to New York, Montreal, and Bermuda became all too common. The Faculty remained in blissful ignorance of this new definition of liberty until it was called to their attention by a careless student and his irate father. The lad had left Cambridge for the more genial climate of Havana, writing a series of post-dated letters, which his chum was supposed to mail to his parents at proper intervals. Unfortunately, his 'goody' [landlady] placed the lot in the mail; the alarmed father came to Cambridge, and no office of the University had the remotest idea where the son might be. Shortly after, the Overseers offered the Faculty the choice between holding a daily morning roll-call and checking attendance in classes. They chose the latter.[40]

We may never know where this story ultimately originated (I doubt that Harvard was the place) or by what means it made its way into missionary lore, where through repeated tellings its narrators dropped any reference to Harvard and reshaped the story, probably unconsciously, to reflect the circumstances of its new environment and to be considered by the missionaries as a true story. It may be more profitable to turn our attention to why, from the world of story existing all around them, the missionaries borrowed and adapted this particular story and then made it perhaps the most popular story in the missionary canon.

As in the bishop and the building fund narrative and the J. Golden Kimball stories, the characters in the unauthorized-trip stories act in ways contrary to what is permissible in their society and can in no way be said to mirror acceptable missionary behavior. In discussing the contribution made to the stability of a social group by the stories members of the group tell each other, anthropologist A.R. Radcliffe-Brown has argued that members of a society share a "system of sentiments" (about right and wrong and about the order of the universe) and that it is the continuance of these collective sentiments that makes the survival of a society possible. The function of folklore, he says is "through regular and adequate expression" to keep these sentiments alive in the minds of the people.[41] The stories discussed in the first part of this paper fit rather neatly into Radcliffe-Brown's formula, supporting, as they do, established church teachings and beliefs. But it would seem that stories like those about the bishop and the building fund, about J. Golden Kimball, and about wayward missionaries would keep sentiments alive in the minds of the people that, if converted into actions, might very well lead to the instability and destruction of the society.

The issue raised here has long intrigued folklorists: Why do members of a social group tell and usually enjoy certain stories whose characters commit deeds the narrators themselves would not engage in nor condone? In her study of the Zuni, Ruth Benedict explained the taboo against polygamy and the simultaneous recurrence of polygamy in Zuni tales in this way: "In the pueblos [where polygamy is strictly forbidden] polygamy is a grandiose folkloristic convention partaking on the one hand of usual mythological exaggeration and on the other of a compensatory daydream." Other violations in Zuni narratives of the tribe's cultural taboos, she said, "must be explained as fundamentally compensatory."[42] In other words, what one could not do because of cultural prohibitions one could experience and relish vicariously through telling stories in which violation of the taboo was a common occurrence.

Benedict's theory goes a long way toward explaining the popularity of Mormon stories whose characters violate accepted Mormon norms. Most of us live willingly in an authoritarian church and have no desire to undercut our leaders, whom we genuinely do respect. Still, it is not particularly easy always to submit one's own will to those in authority. So in a J. Golden Kimball storytelling session some participants take vicarious pleasure in J. Golden's getting the best of these fearsome authorities.

The same principle holds true in the accounts of missionaries' unauthorized trips. Most missionaries are serious and dedicated young people who want to obey mission rules. Still, having once been free to range widely over the countryside in their parents' vehicles, being confined to a restricted space unable, without permission, to travel beyond fixed boundaries can be a chafing experience. These stories serve two main functions. First, since the misdeeds of the errant missionaries are almost always discovered and the rule breakers are either sent home or disciplined in some other ways, the stories play a cautionary role demonstrating to others who might like to take their own trips that they really can't get away with anything. In fact, according to one former missionary, his mission president used to tell the unauthorized trip story to his missionaries to make just that point.[43] Second, and more important, the stories play the compensatory role discussed by Ruth Benedict, allowing the missionaries to participate vicariously in actions otherwise denied them. For example, one returned missionary, who had served as assistant to the mission president, told me: "You would always like to do something like that yourself, and you kinda admire some someone who has the guts to do it." Another returned missionary, also a former assistant to his mission president, said, very perceptively, "Those of us who were straight, who strictly followed the mission code of conduct, had to tell stories like these in order to continue working. In words not too unlike those of these two returned missionaries, folklorist Roger Abrahams typifies a folk type similar to the errant missionary:

> His actions cannot be interpreted as providing a model for future conduct. He is a projection of desires generally thwarted by society. His celebrated deeds function as an approved steam-valve for the group; he is allowed to function in this basically childish way so that the group may vicariously live his adventures without actually acting on his impulses. To encourage such action would be to place the existence of the group in jeopardy.[44]

In other words, the stories provide the narrators and their audience the pleasure of sin without having to suffer its consequences. More seriously, they serve the useful function of contributing to the social cohesion Radcliffe-Brown talks about, making it easier for the missionaries to relieve the societal pressures and tensions that inhibit their natural inclinations and that might otherwise be the undoing of both themselves and their group.

Contrary to what might be expected, then, stories of rule (or taboo) violations still serve as a mirror for culture and provide excellent data in our attempts to understand the societies to which we belong. As a mirror for what is most important in a group, folklore reveals not only outward behavior but also inner desires, not only what we can do but also what we might like to do if our society did not decree otherwise. At the same time it provides us the means of coming to terms with our society's strictures and, thereby, of living more comfortably in that society. As we seek in Mormon folklore a reflection of Mormon life, we must be prepared to peer into hearts that are not always pure. Mirrors are pretty truthful: they reveal us as we are, not as we would like to be. Honest research requires us to give a complete picture of the people we study, with both their strengths and their weaknesses. The following story, told about a conflict between a pioneer woman and a Native American, gives an unflattering view of Native Americans, but an even less attractive picture of people who enjoy and tell such stories:

> After the Indians and the white people had become a little friendly, they didn't go to the fort quite as often. This one day there was this girl down in town and she was washing. They lived quite close to the hills and Indians were camped quite close in the foothills. This girl was washing; she had a washing machine that was an old wooden one that had a wheel that would turn. This Indian brave came down and he had long braids. He came down and he started acting smart to her and talking smart to her and she couldn't understand him. He wanted different things that she had at her home; she wouldn't give them to him. When she wouldn't give them to him, he grabbed her and started throwing her around. She grabbed one lock of his hair, his braid, and hurried and put it into the wringer [of the washing machine] and wound it up tight and fixed it so it couldn't run back, and then she turned and fled while he was tied to the wringer.[45]

To the careful researcher this narrative recounts a paradoxical tale: It mirrors a time when Mormon settlers and local Indians lived on the fringes of open hostility toward each other. It captures a continuing Mormon fascination with that time. And it draws in heroic lines a portrait of a typical pioneer woman who bravely and resourcefully faced down a marauding Indian and whose courage can inspire contemporary women facing a new set of dangers in today's society. But, in an age when we supposedly value cultural diversity and practice ethnic tolerance, the narrative also reflects and perpetuates an uncomplimentary and dehumanizing picture of Native Americans. The Native Americans, whose valleys the early Saints moved into, would tell quite different stories of the pioneer settlement. The story serves, therefore, as an unsettling reminder that we have failed to reach our stated ideals (we do not usually ridicule those we consider our equals) and that we have some distance to travel before we overcome old animosities.

One of the least attractive features of Mormon folklore is the inclination to take uncharitable and unChristian pleasure in hearing that God has punished enemies of the church. This same inclination is evident is some of our popular literature. For example, in their book *Carthage Conspiracy*, Dallin H. Oaks and Marvin S. Hill write: "A persistent Utah myth holds that some of the murderers of Joseph and Hyrum Smith met fittingly gruesome deaths—that Providence intervened to dispense the justice denied in the Carthage trial. But the five defendants who went to trial, including men who had been shown to be leaders in the murder plot and others associated with them, enjoyed notably successful careers"[46] The myth Oaks and Hill refer to is that perpetuated principally by N. B. Lundwall's oft-reprinted *The Fate of the Persecutors of the Prophet Joseph Smith*; the popularity of this book suggests, unfortunately, that Mormons are as capable as anyone of taking uncharitable and unChristian pleasure from the discomfort of those who oppose them.[47] This pleasure is evident in numerous folk narratives, like this one:

> There was a preacher in Yakima, Washington, who hated Mormons and the Mormon Church. Because of his constant efforts the man became well known for his feelings. One Sunday he delivered an unusual fiery speech against the Mormon Church in which he denounced Joseph Smith as a liar and the Book of Mormon as a fraud. In his closing remarks he stated that if everything he said wasn't true the Lord should strike him dead. After the services he walked out of the church and fell dead upon the lawn.[48]

This same theme is especially evident in missionary lore in which those who mistreat the missionaries suffer terrible fates. In one account known throughout the mission fields, two missionaries leave their sacred garments in a Laundromat while they go to lunch. In their absence the anti-Mormon proprietor hangs the garments in the window of the establishment with the sign, "See the Mormon Monkey Suits." The missionaries, following Biblical injunction, shake dust from their feet, cursing the place. Shortly afterward the Laundromat burns down with the proprietor inside, the fire so hot it melts the bricks.[49]

Fortunately, most Mormon lore tells a different story. The most neglected stories in Mormon folklore research are narratives that tell of intense service willingly given, of kind and charitable acts performed by church members. There are two reasons for this neglect. First, stories of devoted service are so common place that no one elects to study them. Second, most of the stories studied in the past by folklorists, including me, have focused more on dramatic tales of the supernatural than on less dramatic stories of losing oneself in service, stories that really go to the heart of what it means to be Mormon. Most of the supernatural narratives recount stirring instances in which God or his angels intervene in the lives of church members to save them from spiritual or physical difficulty. Abstracted from the culture that produces them, these supernatural narratives, which certainly do exist, can easily give one the impression that Mormonism is an entirely *me*-centered religion whose members are concerned most with what God can do for them. While it is true that Mormons seek God's help in personal matters, their religion itself is primarily an *other*-centered religion whose members are encouraged to sacrifice their own interests to devote themselves to the service of others.

This service can take many forms, such as missionary and temple work, but I will mention here only humanitarian service, in which members reach out to members and non-members alike to help them in times of spiritual, physical, or financial difficulty. In a recent LDS conference address, Apostle Joseph B. Wirthlin spoke of acts of loving service expected of church members. He stated: "Often the greatest manisfestations of love are the simple acts of kindness and caring we extend to those we meet along the path of life." And he added:

> At the final day the Savior will not ask about the nature of our callings. He will not inquire about our material possessions or fame. He will ask if we ministered to the sick, gave food and drink to the hungry, visited those in prison, or gave succor to the weak. When we reach out to assist the least of Heavenly Father's children, we do it unto Him. That is the essence of the gospel of Jesus Christ.[50]

Once one understands that service is a vital and central part of LDS belief, then those dramatic tales of divine intervention, take on an entirely different character. They can be seen not simply as accounts of how God has helped individuals with their personal problems but as behavioral models urging individuals to help others as God has helped them. One example will have to suffice:

> Her aunt went on a mission in Canada and one night they had to go to a zone conference quite a ways away and the road was just an old road out

in the middle of nowhere. On their way home about midnight right out in the middle of the road their car broke down in the middle of a blizzard. It was practically hailing and the wind was blowing really bad. They didn't know how to fix it and they couldn't walk because of the weather so they sat in the car and prayed. They were getting really cold and all at once this man came up and knocked on their window and asked them if they needed some help. They hadn't heard a car come up, the man was kind of a funny-looking little man. He went and opened up the hood and fixed their car and it just started running great. And before they ever had time to even thank him, he just disappeared.[51]

This story and others of divine help all have what I have called an "if/then" structure. If the Lord's messenger really saved the missionaries from the storm, if the daughter of the woman who had attended the temple was really saved by the deceased woman for whom the mother had just completed vicarious ordinances, if the sister missionaries really were saved from a rapist by three angelic beings—if these events really happened, then missionary and temple work must be true principles; and if they are true principles, then we should diligently pursue them; and if we pursue them, then the Lord will help us become instruments in serving others. He will help us practice what we profess. These are the stories' most important messages.

The LDS church has in recent years expanded its humanitarian efforts, especially in former eastern-block and third-world countries, sending out senior couples not to proselytize but to provide educational, medical, agricultural, and other services. Most folk narratives, however, speak of ordinary members who during the routine of daily life take time out to help others. The following story is typical:

> When we moved here our neighbor, Elmer Henderson was in the late stages of MS. Our priesthood quorum organized itself to care for him. Each day one of us would read to him for a few hours, and each night one of us would help him bathe. A member had built a motorized sling to lift him from his wheelchair into the tub, which a single person could operate with a little training, and that is what we used so he could have a full body bath each day, which helped immensely in avoiding bedsores. This went on for about five years until he died.[52]

Stories of other acts of service tell of Relief Society women in a local congregation taking turns sitting with the ill or dying; of a railroad worker during the great depression who divided his shift with another worker so each could earn enough money to feed his family; of a graduate student at the University of Chicago, who spent his Saturdays tutoring children from disadvantaged homes on Chicago's south side; of a soldier during the Korean War who donated his entire mustering out pay to a Korean orphanage; of a family that spent time each week to prepare food for the homeless; of a scoutmaster who held an incapacitated scout on his shoulders throughout a very long and very hot pioneer days parade; of a financially strapped church member in Finland who rode his bicycle across town early in the morning to clear a frail widow's walkway after each snow storm; of a church member who, upon finding a drunk man lying in his own vomit, picked him up, cleaned him up, and took him to his hotel.[53]

The acts of service described in these stories are certainly not peculiar to Mormons. They are the kinds of actions one hopes each decent human being might undertake when encountering others in distress. For Mormons striving to practice their religion, however, they are centrally important, as they attempt, in the words of one of their hymns, "to wake up and do something more than dream of their mansion above." Though more pedestrian in character than dramatic supernatural tales, these stories take us much closer to the core of Mormon moral and humane values than the supernatural stories ever will. It is my hope that in the future, researchers in Mormon folklore, in trying to understand what makes Mormons tick, will continue to collect the stories I have focused on this evening, and that they will also make a concerted effort to collect and study these more pedestrian stories of service.

Finally, every telling of a story, whether supernatural or not, is in some ways an exercise in behavior modification, an employment by the narrator of a rhetorical strategy designed to persuade the audience to accept a certain point of view or to follow a certain course of action—to convince one's fellows, for example, that ordaining posts to the priesthood is not a very healthy practice. Few storytellers would consider themselves artists, but they know that if they are to encourage the righteous or reform sinners they must make their stories artful—that is, they must imbue them with power. The principal difference between successful oral and written storytelling lies not so much in the artistic merit of the works created but in the methods of composition. The writer achieves artistic power by carefully arranging words on the written page. The teller of tales, in a dynamic process that cannot adequately be captured on the written page, achieves the same end by responding to an active audience. It is this interplay between teller and listeners that in the final analysis, will give shape, meaning, and power to the story created. The art of folklore, therefore, lies not just in the tale told, but in the *telling* of the tale. Many Mormon folk narratives, reduced to paper, may seem fairly flat, but we should remember that in actual performance many have had the power to move listeners to laughter and to tears.

I return now to the question I asked in my title: What is true in Mormon folklore? The answer is, of course, all of it. It will on occasion keep alive the memory of events as they actually occurred. It will always provide a faithful record of what people believe happened in the past and thus will give us insights into the motivations that move these people to action. Above all, it will mirror the culture of the people who possess it, reflecting their hopes, anxieties and fears; their attitudes and beliefs; their means of dealing with the pressures imposed upon them by the societies they live in; their faults and weaknesses; and their desires to serve their fellow beings. If the stories that circulate among members of the LDS church are artfully constructed, artfully told, and artfully listened to, they will have the power, as Sir Philip Sidney informed us over four hundred years ago, to both entertain and instruct, to hold "children from play and old men from the chimney corner."[54] And in some instances, they will move us beyond the borders of Mormondom and teach us what it means to be human. I hope that those charged with developing Mormon Studies programs, in this country and in Europe, will make good use of the folklore in university folklore archives and good use of lore still to be collected. Failing to do so would let pass unnoticed materials crucially important in our efforts to understand Mormon hearts and minds.

NOTES

Unless otherwise noted, all folklore texts referenced in this paper are located in the William A. Wilson Folklore Archive housed in L. Tom Perry Special Collections of the Harold B. Lee Library at Brigham Young University. The texts come from four separate collections. References to the texts begin in each instance with the name of the collector, followed by the date of collection. Following the date, one of the following classifications is given:

(1) field collections, indicated by FA1, followed by the number of the collection and specific page numbers, followed by the title of the project;

(2) the genre collections, numbered FA2 through 11, followed by a text's multiple-digit location number;

(3) the William A. Wilson Three Nephites Collection, indicated as "Nephite Collection" followed by the number of the text; or

(4) the William A. Wilson LDS Missionary Collection, indicated as "Missionary Collection," followed by the number of the text.

1. William A. Wilson, "'We Did Everything Together': Farming Customs of the Mountainwest." *Northwest Folklore* 4 (spring–summer 1985): 23–30.

2. Jon Butler, *Awash in a Sea of Faith: Christianizing the American People* (Cambridge: Harvard University Press, 1990), 83.

3. See for example, Ronald W. Walker, "The Persisting Idea of American Treasure Hunting," *BYU Studies* 24 (fall 1984): 430–31, 435, 443, 450, 452, and D. Michael Quinn, *Early Mormonism and the Magic World View* (Salt Lake City: Signature Books, 1987), much of the book and especially 11, 14, 20, 21.

4. Darlo Tate, collector, 1969, Nephite Collection, 381.

5. Jay Healy, collector, n.d., Nephite Collection, 722,

6. Sterling M. McMurrin, Review of *Early Mormonism and the Magic World View*, by D. Michael Quinn, *Utah Historical Quarterly* 56 (spring 1988): 200.

7. Hector Lee, *The Three Nephites: The Substance and Significance of the Legend in Folklore* (Albuquerque: The University of New Mexico Press, 1949).

8. Leonard J. Arrington, "Myth, Symbol, and Truth," in *Reflections of a Mormon Historian: Leonard J. Arrington on the New Mormon History*, ed. Reid L. Neilson and Ronald W. Walker (Norman, Oklahoma: The Arthur H. Clark Company, 2006), 133.

9. Eric Foner, "My Life as a Historian," in *Who Owns History? Rethinking the Past in a Changing World* (New York: Hill and Want, 2002), 10.

10. Brynjulf Alver, "Historical Legends and Historical Truth," *Nordic Folklore: Recent Studies*, ed. Reimund Kvideland and Henning K. Sehmsdorf, in collaboration with Elizabeth Simpson (Bloomington: Indiana University Press, 1989), 138.

11. David M. Pendergast and Clement W. Meighan, "Folk Traditions as Historical Fact: A Paiute Example," *Journal of American Folklore* 72 (April–June 1959):128–33.

12. David D. Buchan, "History and Harlaw," *Journal of the Folklore Institute* 5 (1968): 58–67.

13. Alver, 139.

14. Charles William Ryan, collector, 1970, FA7 6.6.2.8.1.

15. Reynol E. Bowman, collector, 1972, FA1 169, "The Invasion of 1970: The Mormon Conspiratorial Mind."

16. Franz Boas, *Tsimshian Mythology*, Thirty-First Annual Report of the Bureau of American Ethnology, Accompanying Paper (Washington, D.C.: Government Printing Office, 1916), 393.
17. William A. Wilson, "Folklore as History: Facts amid the Legends," *Utah Historical Quarterly* 41 (winter 1973): 48–49.
18. Barre Toelken, *The Dynamics of Folklore* (Boston: Houghton Mifflin Company, 1979), 24.
19. See Robert McCarl, *Good Fire/Bad Night: A Cultural Sketch of the District of Columbia Fire Fighters as Seen through their Occupational Folklife* (Washington, D.C.: District of Columbia Fire Fighters Association, Local 36, 1980).
20. John B. Harris and William A. Wilson, collectors, 1968, Missionary Collection 56.
21. Mary Stewart, collector, 1976, FA2 1.1.3.2.2.1.
22. Gregory Vernon, collector, 1969, FA1 427:53–62, "Missionary Stories,"
23. As told to me during a telephone conversation with Leonard J. Arrington, following Arrington's lecture, 26 February 1987.
24. From Zora Neale Hurston, *Mules and Men*, Perennial Library edition (1935; repr., New York: Harper & Row, 1990), 88–89.
25. From tape recorded interview with Woodruff Thompson in Provo, Utah, n.d. Tape in possession of William A. Wilson.
26. For examples, see Richard M. Dorson, *American Negro Folktales* (Bloomington: Indiana University Press, 1958), 124–71.
27. Terrie Leishman, collector, 1978, Missionary Collection 2241.
28. Douglas Airmet, collector, n.d., Missionary Collection 774.
29. Jane England, collector, 1990, Missionary Collection 3398.
30. S. Robinson, collector, 1992, included in correspondence from William Lightfoot to William A. Wilson.
31. Laura Anderson, collector, 1990, Missionary Collection 3480.
32. Rhonda Jones, collector, 1992, Missionary Collection 3476.
33. Ruth Benedict, *Zuni Mythology*, 2 vols. (New York City: Columbia University Press, 1935), 1:xv, xxx.
34. ibid, 1:xiii.
35. ibid, 1:xv–xvi.
36. Norman Ray Frei, collector, 1969, FA1 237:88, "Mormon Humor." .
37. Ibid, 237:38. For discussions of J. Golden Kimball as a Mormon folk hero, see William A. Wilson, "The Paradox of Mormon Folklore, *BYU Studies* 17 (autumn 1976):52–55, and Eric A. Eliason, *The J. Golden Kimball Stories* (Urbana: University of Illinois Press, 2007).
38. Sheral Hyde, collector, 1978, Missionary Collection 3030.
39. Charles William Ryan, collector, 1971, Missionary Collection 585.
40. Samuel Eliot Morison, *Three Centuries of Harvard, 1636–1936* (Cambridge: Harvard University Press, 1937), 368–69.
41. A.R. Radcliffe-Brown, "The Interpretation of Andamanese Customs and Beliefs: Myths and Legends," in *The Andaman Islanders* (Cambridge: Oxford University Press, 1922), 376–405.
42. Benedict, 1:xvi.
43. Debra Pearson, collector, 1982, Missionary Collection 3806; see also Sheral Hyde, collector, 1978, Missionary Collection 3816.
44. Roger C. Abrahams, "Some Varieties of Heroes in America," *Journal of the Folklore Institute* 3 (1966):341–42.
45. Doris Blackham and Susan Christensen, collectors, 1971, FA4 3.2.1.5.2.2.1.
46. Dallin H. Oaks and Marvin S. Hill, *Carthage Conspiracy: The Trial of the Accused Assassins of Joseph Smith* (Urbana: University of Illinois Press, 1975), 217.
47. N. B. Lundwall, *The Fate of the Persecutors of the Prophet Joseph Smith* (Salt Lake City: n.p., 1952).
48. Kalvin Miller, collector, 1961, FA2 1.4.6.1.
49. Shelley Rygg, collector, 1975, Missionary Collection 889. The archive contains sixty-seven versions of this story from mission fields around the world.

50. Joseph B. Wirthlin, "The Great Commandment," *Ensign* 37 (November 2007): 29–30.
51. Cindy Brough, collector, 1978, Nephite Collection 1452.
52. Eugene England to William A. Wilson, 1998, letter in possession of Wilson.
53. The examples cited in this paragraph are drawn from narratives I have heard all of my life growing up and living in Mormon society. They are typical of many such stories told throughout the LDS church but seldom recorded.
54. Sir Philip Sidney, "An Apology for Poetry," in *Renaissance England: Poetry and Prose from the Reformation to the Restoration*, ed. Roy Lamson and Hallett Smith (New York: W.W. Norton, 1956), 285.